Nelson

Spelling

Developing Skills

John Jackman

BOOK ONE

Scottish Adviser: Iain Campbell

CONTENTS/SCOPE AND SEQUENCE

Page	Focus	Extra	Extension	Focus resource	Extension resource
4/5 Flashback	*Flashback*	*Flashback*	*Flashback*	*Flashback*	*Flashback*
6/7 Unit 1 ain air	-ain endings	-air -are homophones	-air compound words	-ain -air pattern/ word building	using -air -are -ere -ear homophones
8/9 Unit 2 ff ll ss	identifying missing double letters	plurals -ss + es	+ ing (doubling final consonant)	-ell -ill -ess -oss patterns/rime	+ ing (doubling final consonant)
10/11 Unit 3 un dis de re pre	selecting prefixes	identifying prefixes	dictionary work - finding prefixes	practising un dis de re pre patterns; un- fan (building)	using prefix un-
12/13 Unit 4 le endings	rhyming sets; using -le words	-le + ed	-ubble and -ouble	-ddle -angle -umble patterns/ word building	crossword; jumbled letter puzzle
14/15 Unit 5 a-e ai ay	selecting a-e/ai/ay words	a-e ai ay + ing	-ace -age	-ain -ake -ay patterns/word building	-ail -ame -ay -ave patterns/jumbled letters puzzle
16/17 Unit 6 i-e igh y	using y	y + ed	igh comparatives and superlatives	igh pattern; ight fan (building)	igh + ly words; igh homophones
18/19 Unit 7 o-e oa ow	o-e oa ow rhyming words	different ow sounds	silent k	-oad -ow -ope patterns; -ow -oke -oat word building	different ow sounds/ homographs
20/21 Unit 8 wh	wh question words	words within wh words	compound words	wh pattern; wh- fan (building)	using *what who whose*; wh word puzzle
22/23 Unit 9 st str	finding st- str- words	st- str- words puzzle	vowels and consonants	st- str- pattern/ word building	alphabetical ordering
24/25 Unit 10 dictionary work	letter puzzle	ordering letters; simple alphabetical order	alphabetical ordering by 2nd letter	alphabet activities	alphabetical ordering (1st/ 2nd letter) homonyms
26/27 Check-up 1	*Check-up 1*	*Check-up 1*	*Check-up 1*	*Check-up 1*	*Check-up 1*
28/29 Unit 11 less ful ly	selecting suffixes	y + ly	using suffixes	-less pattern/fan (building); -fully fan (building)	using -less -fully
30/31 Unit 12 er ir ur	er ir ur rhyming words	+ er (doubling final consonant)	word search; +ing	-er fan (building)	+ er + ed +ing (doubling final consonant)
32/33 Unit 13 compound words	making simple compound words	more compound words	identifying compound words	*some any every* compound words	making/analysing compound words

Page	Focus	Extra	Extension	Focus resource	Extension resource
34/35 Unit 14 some y endings	cloze; rhyming y words	+ y (doubling final consonant)	e + y	-y fan (building adjectives)	+ y (doubling final consonant/dropping final e/changing y to i)
36/37 Unit 15 er est	weather adjectives	y + er	y + est	-er -est fans (building adjectives)	+er +est (doubling final consonant/dropping final e/changing y to i)
38/39 Unit 16 sp spr	identifying sp spr words	sp spr wordsearch	vowel letters	sp- spr- patterns/ word building	synonyms with sp- spr-; using a dictionary
40/41 Unit 17 making plurals	+s	-s, -x, -ch, -sh plurals	consonant/y and vowel/y plurals	's' 'es' plurals	consonant/y and vowel/y plurals
42/43 Unit 18 silent b and k	identifying silent letters	silent b + suffix	silent k + suffix	-mb kn- patterns/ word building	identifying silent letters
44/45 Unit 19 silent w	silent w wordsearch	word webs	more silent letters	w- fan (building)	identifying silent letters
46/47 Check-up 2	*Check-up 2*	*Check-up 2*	*Check-up 2*	*Check-up 2*	*Check-up 2*
48/49 Unit 20 one ome ove	rhyming words	-e +ing	different 'o' sounds	-one ove -ome -ive patterns/ rime	different 'o' sounds
50/51 Unit 21 words in words	finding hidden words	sets of words in words	pictorial mnemonics	colouring hidden words	sets of words in words
52/53 Unit 22 aw or ore oor au	aw verbs +ing	definitions puzzle	homophones	-aw fan (building)	aw au or oor oar our homophones
54/55 Unit 23 nch tch	rhyming words	tch verbs	nch tch plurals	-tch -nch patterns/ rime	selecting -tch -nch; 'es' plurals
56/57 Unit 24 shortened words	exploding contractions	creating contractions	possible confusions	making simple contractions	making/using more advanced contractions using it's and its
58/59 Unit 25 mis con ex co anti	prefixes + roots	defining words with prefixes	dictionary research	mis non ex co anti patterns; mis- fan (building)	mis ex anti non wordsearch
60/61 Unit 26 ou	rhyming words	ou contractions	alphabetical order; definitions	-ound fan (building)	using *could should would*; ou homophones
62/64 Check-up 3	*Check-up 3*	*Check-up 3*	*Check-up 3*	*Check-up 3*	*Check-up 3*

 OCUS

A Find the missing letters. Copy the words into your book.

1 c _ k _

2 f _ v _

3 ___ ick

4 b ___ k

5 c ___ t

6 b ___

7 d ___ n

8 m ___ se

B What are these? Write the words into your book.

1

2

3

4

5

6

7

8

9

10

11

12

 **XTRA**

A Write the answers to these word sums.

1 drive + ing =   **2** try + ing =   **3** chase + ed =

4 help + ful =   **5** happy + ly =   **6** beauty + ful =

B Write a word that has the same spelling pattern and rhymes with:

1 down   **2** mouse   **3** might   **4** roast   **5** screw   **6** dark

7 book   **8** joint   **9** blow   **10** toy   **11** weather   **12** shower

 **XTENSION**

A Write these words in alphabetical order.

1 hood   wood   good   food

2 clue   crew   cart   choose   coin

B Sort the words in the box into two lists.

| show   shower   blower   clown   window   tower   drowning |
| rower   snowing   own   know   lower   brown   bowler   how |

<u>ow</u> sounds like <u>ow</u> in <u>owl</u>	<u>ow</u> sounds like <u>o</u> in h<u>o</u>me

C Make the antonym of each of these words by adding the prefix **un** or **dis**.

1 happy   **2** appear   **3** trust   **4** kind

D Copy these sentences using the correct word.

1 Where shall I meet/meat you?

2 The shop is having a sail/sale.

3 Have you combed your hare/hair?

ain
air

The **rain** in Sp**ain** stays m**ain**ly on the pl**ain**.

KEY WORDS

rain
train
strain
sprain
brain
drain
grain
stain
chain

air
pair
chair
stairs

A Look at these picture clues.
Write the **ain** words in your book.

1 t_____   2 st_____

3 ch_____   4 dr_____

B Write six other **ain** key words neatly in your book.

C Look at the rhyme at the top of the page.
Write the words that have the **ain** pattern.

Find the pairs of homophones in the puzzle box.

Remember, **homophones** sound the same but are spelt differently.

f	s	t	a	i	r	s
n	i	o	p	f	h	u
u	t	g	p	a	i	r
k	l	h	e	i	d	g
d	f	h	a	r	e	b
s	t	a	r	e	s	m
d	f	i	b	v	q	n
f	a	r	e	d	v	g

Remember, **compound words** are words which are made from two smaller words.

The answers to these clues are all compound words which have the **air** letter pattern.

1 I cut and wash hair.
2 This is where aeroplanes land and take off.
3 Another name for an aeroplane.
4 The opposite of upstairs.
5 Lots of fun rides.
6 You will feel comfortable sitting in this.

ff ll
ss

Tess ate fluff
Tess ate jelly,
Tess went home
With a pain in her belly!

Focus

KEY WORDS

off
puff
cliff
tell
sell
smell
spell
fill
frill
grill
dress
press
cross

What are they doing?
Write the words in your book.
Don't forget the **ing**.

1 s____ing   2 f____ing   3 d____ing

DING DONG!

4 p____ing   5 s____ing   6 c____ing

Write a sentence about one of the pictures.

Remember, to make the plural of most nouns we just add **s**.

one cliff   two cliff**s**

But if the word ends with **ss** we add **es**.

one dress   two dress**es**

 Write the plurals of these words.

1 *frill* 2 *farm* 3 *smell* 4 *car* 5 *puff*

B Write the plurals of these words.

1 *mess* 2 *press* 3 *grass* 4 *cross* 5 *kiss*

EXTENSION

Sometimes we double the last letter before we add **ing**, like this:

bat   ba**tt**ing   shop   sho**pp**ing

and sometimes we don't, like this:

sing   sin**g**ing   read   rea**d**ing

Look at the letter before the last letter.
Is it just one vowel (**a e i o u**)?

b<u>a</u>t	yes	b<u>a</u>**tt**ing
sh<u>o</u>p	yes	sh<u>o</u>**pp**ing
s<u>i</u>ng	no, **n** is not a vowel	s<u>i</u>n**g**ing
r<u>ea</u>d	no, there are two vowels	r<u>ea</u>**d**ing

Be careful!
This doesn't work for
words ending in **w**, **x**
or **y**.

Can you work out when the last letter is doubled?
Add **ing** to these words. The underlines will help you.

1 *h<u>o</u>p* 2 *w<u>i</u>n* 3 *s<u>i</u>t* 4 *g<u>e</u>t* 5 *sl<u>a</u>p*

6 *p<u>u</u>t* 7 *a<u>s</u>k* 8 *st<u>o</u>p* 9 *wi<u>s</u>h* 10 *spe<u>ll</u>*

11 *cl<u>a</u>p* 12 *wa<u>l</u>k* 13 *bl<u>o</u>w* 14 *b<u>o</u>x* 15 *pl<u>a</u>y*

un
dis de
re pre

Don't **dis**obey,
Don't **dis**agree.
Your room is **un**tidy.
Clean it up by tea!

FOCUS

KEY WORDS

untidy
untie
unwell
dislike
disobey
disagree
decode
defuse
refill
revisit
preset
preview

Add **un** or **dis** to make the opposites of these words.
The pictures will help you.

1 ___well   2 ___like   3 ___tidy

4 ___agree   5 ___tie   6 ___obey

Write a sentence about one of the pictures.

A **prefix** is a group of letters at the beginning of a word that changes the meaning.

These are some important prefixes.

well **un**well   mist **de**mist   like **dis**like
build **re**build   fix **pre**fix

Copy these words and underline the prefixes.

1 unpopular   2 depress   3 disqualify

4 revisit   5 prejudge   6 unzip

7 decode   8 disappear   9 replay

10 preview   11 unhelpful   12 prehistoric

Prefix has a p<u>re</u>fix!

XTENSION

A Use a dictionary to help you to write three other words beginning with each of the five prefixes **un**, **dis**, **de**, **re**, and **pre**. The first is done to help you.

1 **un**   unlucky   unseen   unhappy

B Write a sentence to explain what you think each prefix means.

le

endings

Double, double, toil and trouble;
Fire burn and cauldron bubble.

Macbeth William Shakespeare

FOCUS

KEY WORDS

candle
handle
paddle
middle

angle
bangle
rectangle
jingle
single

jumble
tumble
crumble
grumble

A Copy these groups of words.
Underline the one with the different letter pattern.

1 single jingle candle tingle

2 jumble middle grumble crumble

3 bangle handle rectangle tangle

B What am I?
Look at the picture clues and complete the sentences.
Then write the key word that matches the clue.
The first one is done to help you.

1 Light me up with a . *candle*

2 You need me to row a

3 Mum broke me off the .

4 I am worn on your  .

5 I have four .

EXTRA

Remember, a **verb** is a doing or being word.

We add **ed** to a verb if the action has happened in the **past**, and we add **ing** if it is happening at the **present** time.

Copy the table, then add **ing** and **ed** to each verb.
The first is done to help you.
Remember what happens if the verb ends with **e**.

verb	present	past
grumble	grumbling	grumbled
fumble		
crumble		
jingle		
scramble		
tumble		

EXTENSION

couple	bubble
trouble	rubble
double	stubble

The two sets of **le** words in the box have similar sounds, but different letter patterns.

A Copy the words, underlining the silent letter in three of the words.

B Write sentences using four of the words.

a-e
ai ay

It's **ace** to pl**ay** in the r**ai**n!

KEY WORDS

ace
lace
place
pace
space
age
page
stage
pay
pray
spray
rain
train
strain

A Write the word in your book that matches each picture.

1 r**ai**n or tr**ai**n 2 r**ace** or p**ace** 3 r**age** or c**age**

4 pr**ay** or spr**ay** 5 r**ace** or l**ace** 6 p**age** or r**age**

B Write three words that rhyme with **ace**.

C Write three words that rhyme with **age**.

> Remember, when we add **ing** to a word ending in **e**, we have to leave off the **e**.

Do these word sums in your book.

1 shake + ing =
2 wake + ing =
3 rake + ing =
4 play + ing =
5 say + ing =
6 spray + ing =
7 sail + ing =
8 claim + ing =
9 strain + ing =
10 trace + ing =
11 space + ing =
12 brace + ing =

EXTENSION

ace and **age** are important spelling patterns.
Notice that when **c** or **g** come before **e** they usually make a soft sound, like a **s** and **j**.

1. Write four words than rhyme with **ace** and have the *ace* spelling pattern.
2. Write four words than rhyme with **age** and have the *age* spelling pattern.
3. Read these words. Listen to the sound of the letter **c**.
    Sort the words into two lists.

package	December	clay	claim	conceal	magnificent
magic	parcel	caterpillar	centre	saucer	horrific

c sounds like s in bus	c sounds like k in pick

i-e
igh y

FOCUS

KEY WORDS

fly
sky
spy
shy
cycle
python
sigh
sight
fight
flight
right
bright
side
slide

A Find a word that ends in **y** to match each picture.
Write the words in your book.

1 c_____   2 f_____   3 d_____

4 f_____   5 s_____   6 s_____

B Write a fun sentence using the words **python** and **cycle**.

EXTRA

If something has happened in the **past**, we add **ed** to the verb.
What has happened to the letter **y** in these words?

cry + ed = cried
fry + ed = fried

If we add **ed** to a small word that ends with **y** we change the **y** to **i** and add **ed**.

What did they do?
Copy these sentences. Choose a word to fill the gaps.
The words in brackets will give you a clue.

1 The toddler (cry) when she fell over.
2 I (try) hard to win the race.
3 Mum (fry) the chips in hot fat.
4 Our clothes (dry) quickly in the hot sun.
5 I (spy) our kitten stealing some cream.

EXTENSION

Adjectives are describing words. Sometimes we make special comparing adjectives by adding **er** or **est**.

A Copy this box and fill in the missing words.
The first one is done for you.

high	higher	highest
light		
tight		
bright		

B Now add *fine, wide* and *wise* to your table. Check your work in a dictionary. What do you notice happens when you add **er** and **est** to words that end in **e**?

17

UNIT 7

o-e
oa
ow

Toad strode along the road.
He followed the mole who lives in a hole.

FOCUS

KEY WORDS

float
goal
groan
moan
foam
broke
rope
hope
note
vote
code
hollow
borrow
tomorrow

A Write two **oa** words that rhyme with each of these words.

1 **mole** rhymes with  goal coal

2 **smoke** rhymes with

3 **vote** rhymes with

4 **dome** rhymes with

B Write two **o-e** words that rhyme with each of these words.

1 soap   2 cloak   3 goat   4 road

18

Sort the words in the box into two lists. Two are done to help you.

Notice that two words can go into both lists.

frown	borrow	tomorrow	drown	bow
hollow	fowl	snowfall	row	window
know	town	known	crown	bowler

ow sounds like ow in how	ow sounds like o in dome
frown	borrow

XTENSION

Silent letters can cause spelling problems!

The letter **k** is silent in **k**now and **k**nown.
The words in the box all have a **silent k**.

| know | knot | knock | knitting | knob | knife |

A Copy the words in the box. Neatly underline the silent letter in each word.

B Write these sentences. Use words from the box to fill the gaps.

1 There was a _____ on the door.
2 Gran didn't _____ who it was.
3 She put down her _____ .
4 The wool got tangled and made a _____ .
5 "I'll have to cut it with this _____ ," she said.

wh

Where is the whale?

KEY WORDS

when
where
wheel
wheat
which
whip
while
white
why
what
who
whose
whole

Copy these questions.
Choose **wh** key words to fill the gaps.

1 _____ are we going?

2 _____ will the bus come?

3 _____ bus are we catching?

4 _____ isn't Dean coming with us?

How many small words can you find in these **wh** words?
For example: where   he (w**he**re); her (w**her**e); here (w**here**).
Now try these. Use the picture for help.

1 wheel   2 white   3 wheat

4 when   5 whisper   6 whisk

7 whimper   8 wherever   9 whirlwind

EXTENSION

Make as many compound words as you can using these words.
The first one is done to help you.

It's usual **not** to make
a compound word of
no one.

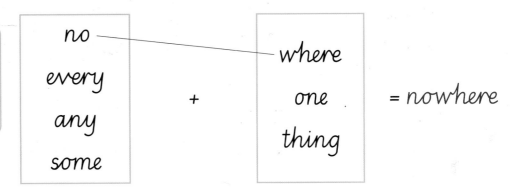

Write three sentences using one word from each of the groups you
have made.

st
str

Start running home – there's a strong storm coming and the stream might overflow!

 FOCUS

KEY WORDS

stall
star
start
stay
steam
steep
still
stop
stray
stream
street
string
strong

Copy the key words neatly into your book.
Tick the ones you can find in the picture.

Lots of words beginning with **st** and **str** are hidden in this puzzle.
Some go across the page and some go down.
Write them in your book.

How did you do?
10 = good
12 or more = brilliant!

s	t	a	y	s	t	i	l	l	p	z	w
t	h	u	s	t	a	r	s	t	a	r	t
e	s	t	r	e	e	t	s	t	r	a	y
a	x	e	b	e	s	t	r	o	n	g	t
m	s	t	o	p	r	s	t	r	i	p	e

Write three sentences. In each sentence include at least one of the
words you have found.

Remember, **a**, **e**, **i**, **o** and **u** are the five **vowel** letters.
All the other letters are called **consonants**.

A In your book draw two boxes.
Sort this jumble of letters.
Put the vowels in one box and the consonants in the other.

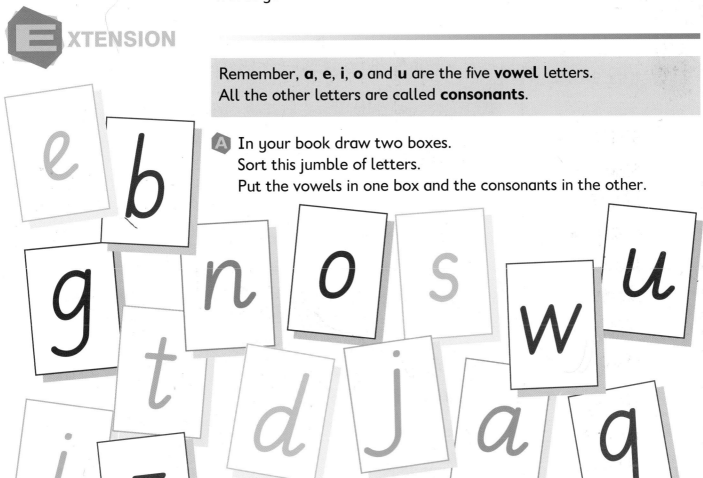

B Write some words using just these letters.
Underline the vowels in each word.
How many words have you made that do not have a vowel?

dictionary work

KEY WORDS

letters
words
vowel
consonant
order
first
last
between
after
next
alphabet
alphabetical
dictionary

a b c d e f g h i j k l m n o p q r s t u v w x y z

Remember, there are 26 letters in the alphabet. Five of the letters are called **vowels**. The rest are called **consonants**.

Write the answers to these questions in your book.

What is:

1 the first letter?

2 the last letter?

3 the letter after **g**?

4 the letter after **s**?

5 the letter before **m**?

6 the letter before **d**?

7 Which comes first, **f** or **k**?

8 Which comes first, **j** or **v**?

9 Which letter is between **l** and **n**?

10 Is **u** nearer to **g** or **z**?

11 Which letter is between **d** and **f**?

12 Is **e** nearer to **b** or **m**?

13 Which two letters are nearest to the middle of the alphabet?

14 Which is the middle vowel letter?

15 Which is the last vowel letter?

16 Which consonants come between the first two vowel letters?

17 Which consonants come between the last two vowel letters?

 **XTRA**

Alphabetical order means the letters are put in the order of the letters in the alphabet.

A Write each of these groups of letters in alphabetical order.

1 h a c e 2 d t k z 3 B S K L
4 G J P R A 5 m j d y s 6 p f a q v d

The words in a dictionary are in alphabetical order. Words starting with **a** come first, words starting with **b** come second, words starting with **c** come third, and so on.

B Write each of these groups of words in alphabetical order.

1 bee cat ant
2 baby apple dog cow
3 house lion fire
4 jelly party games cake

 **XTENSION**

Remember, to put words that all begin with the same letter into alphabetical order you need to look at the second letter of each word.

aeroplane ant apple axe

Write the words in each of these groups in the order they would be in a dictionary.

1 home help hut
2 wood water when will
3 bed brother boy back
4 not name next night

OCUS

What are these? The first letters will give you a clue.
Write the words in your book.

1 r _____   2 c _____   3 c _____   4 s _____

5 c _____   6 s _____   7 f _____   8 f _____

9 s _____   10 s _____   11 w _____   12 s _____

Write sentences about three of the pictures.

A Copy these sentences using the correct word.

1 Can we go to the fare/fair tonight?

2 I've got a new pear/pair of shoes.

3 I don't no/know the answer.

B Write the plural of these words.

1 bell   2 kiss   3 shell   4 dress

C Write the answers to these word sums.

1 walk + ing =   2 bat + ing =   3 scramble + ing =

4 cry + ing =   5 cry + ed =   6 try + ed =

D Make another word from each of these words by adding the prefix **un**, **dis**, **de**, **re** or **pre**.

1 mist   2 zip   3 build   4 view   5 qualify

EXTENSION

A Make a compound word by adding a word from the box to each of these words.

fair   where   chair   air   hair

1 every   2 dresser   3 fun   4 arm   5 craft

B 1 Copy this sentence into your book and circle the vowel letters.

My dad said it was going to be sunny and dry by lunchtime.

2 Which letter sometimes appears in words in place of a vowel?

C 1 Write three words than rhyme with **ace** and have the ace spelling pattern.

2 Write three words than rhyme with **age** and have the age spelling pattern.

D Write these words in alphabetical order.

1 heavy   how   happen   2 never   night   nappy   nothing

less
ful ly

fearless

fearful

fearfully

 FOCUS

KEY WORDS

weekly
kindly
likely
friendly

wishful
hopeful
painful
forgetful

careless
homeless
speechless
fearless

Add **ly**, **ful** or **less** to make these words.
Write the words in your book.

1 *friend____*

2 *pain____*

3 *fear____*

4 *home____*

5 *care____*

6 *forget____*

EXTRA

A group of letters added to the end of a word is called a **suffix**.

Remember, if a word ends in **y**, change the **y** to **i** before adding **ful**, **less** or **ly**, like this:

hap**y** + ly = hap**i**ly

A Join these root words and suffixes, changing the **y** to **i** if you need to. Write them in your book.

1 happy + ly =   2 beauty + ful =

3 pity + less =   4 plenty + ful =

5 mercy + less =   6 merry + ly =

B Write a sentence using two of the words you have made.

EXTENSION

Adding different suffixes to a word can change its meaning.
Use the suffixes in the box to make as many new words as you can using these root words. The first one is done to help you.

ly	ful	less	er	able	ed	ing

1 help   helpless   helpful   helping
          helped   helper   helpfully

2 wish   3 care   4 sink

5 pain   6 friend   7 walk

er
ir ur

Desert island –
thirsty work.
Great pleasure –
found the treasure!

FOCUS

KEY WORDS

germ
term
serve
swerve
butter
gutter
skirt
shirt
first
thirst
nurse
purse
measure
treasure

A Look at the pictures.
Write the rhyming key words.
The first one is done to help you.

1 **serve** rhymes with  *swerve*

2 **gutter** rhymes with

3 **skirt** rhymes with

4 **nurse** rhymes with

5 **measure** rhymes with

B Write in your book five other words that end with **er**.

C Write a sentence that has at least two of the key words in it.

XTRA

er is often a **suffix**.

Remember in short words we must sometimes double the last letter before we add the **er** suffix.

| run | runner | dig | digger |

Look at the letter before the last letter.
Is it just one vowel (**a e i o u**)?

run	yes		runner
shop	yes		shopper
sing	no, **n** is not a vowel		singer
read	no, there are two vowels		reader

Add **er** to these words. The underlines will help you.

1 s_it   2 w_in   3 fl_ip   4 sw_im

5 sp_in   6 ta_nk   7 st_op   8 fi_sh

9 lo_ud   10 we_ak   11 wa_lk   12 wr_ap

XTENSION

A Hidden in the puzzle box are seven **ur** words, seven **ir** words and seven **er** words. Copy them into your book.

s	r	u	b	b	e	r	s	t	i	r	g
i	f	s	k	i	r	t	p	u	r	s	e
r	q	h	u	r	t	e	i	r	e	f	r
m	f	i	z	d	j	m	n	n	v	i	m
n	u	r	s	e	l	p	n	x	e	r	l
t	r	t	e	r	m	e	e	u	r	s	f
s	h	o	p	p	e	r	r	r	s	t	i
m	e	a	s	u	r	e	p	n	e	z	r

Think whether you need to drop the final **e** before adding **ing**.

B Add **ing** to four of the words and write four sentences using your new words.

compound words

playground   **playtime**

KEY WORDS

someone
somebody
something
somewhere

anyone
anybody
anything
anywhere

everyone
everybody
everything
everywhere

Copy and finish these word sums.
Write the answers in your book.

1 paint + brush =

2 earth + worm =

3 foot + ball =

4 egg + cup =

5 goal + keeper =

6 tool + box =

Remember, when two words are joined, the new word is called a **compound word**.

Write as many compound words as you can that have these as part of the words.

1 body   2 thing   3 eye   4 no

5 day   6 time   7 green   8 foot

9 way   10 grand   11 path   12 post

 XTENSION

1 Copy the compound words in this postcard.

Dear Grandmother,
We are having fun here at the seaside, making sandcastles and playing football. At lunchtime we walk up the footpath and have beefburgers or fishfingers at the cafe.
Your loving grandson,
Josh

Mrs Greensmith
Windmill House
Woodland Road
Southend
SD43 5SN

2 Write some compound words you might find at the supermarket. Use the picture to help you.

some y endings

stormy
windy
grumpy
chilly
cheeky
dirty

KEY WORDS

chilly
frilly
windy
happy
frosty
dusty
lucky
rainy
sleepy
cheeky
stormy
dirty
grumpy

A Look at the picture.
Copy and finish each sentence with a key word.

1 It was a r_____ day.

2 I was feeling g_____ .

3 Jenny was smiling and looking h_____ .

4 "It is l_____ I planted the seeds yesterday," she said.

B Find a key word to rhyme with:

1 nappy   2 rusty   3 lumpy   4 mucky

EXTRA

Remember, **nouns** are naming words and **adjectives** are describing words.

Nouns can be made into adjectives by adding **y**, like this:

rain   a rain**y** day

But remember, if the letter before the last is a single vowel (**a e i o u**), double the last letter, like this:

m**u**d   mu**dd**y clothes

A Copy these nouns and add **y** to make them into adjectives.

1 flash   2 wind   3 rock   4 luck   5 rust
6 fog   7 sun   8 fun   9 spot   10 sleep

B Write three sentences, each using at least one of the words you have made.

EXTENSION

To make an adjective with a **y** from a word ending in **e**, remember to drop the **e**, like this:

slim~~e~~ + y   slim**y**

Copy and complete this chart.

noun	adjective
wave	wavy
laze	
bone	
	rosy
smoke	
	stony

er
est

muddy

muddier

muddiest

FOCUS

KEY WORDS

windy
windier
windiest

foggy
foggier
foggiest

sunny
sunnier
sunniest

rainy
rainier
rainiest

A Look at these weather pictures.
Write the key words in your book.

1 w_____

2 f_____

3 s_____

4 r_____

B Copy into your book all the key words that have double letters.

If we want to turn an adjective that ends in **y** into a special adjective to compare **two** things, we change the **y** to **i** and add **er**, like this:

My friend is funn**y**.   She is funn**ier** than me.

Fill in the blanks by making a comparing adjective from the word in bold. The first one is done to help you.

1 **windy**   It is *windier* than it was yesterday.

2 **chilly**   I am feeling a lot _____ than I was at home.

3 **stormy**   It was _____ last night than on Friday.

4 **cloudy**   It is _____ now than it was this morning.

**XTENSION**

If we want to turn an adjective that ends in **y** into a special adjective to compare **more than two** things, we change the **y** to **i** and add **est**, like this:

My friend is funn**y**.   She is the funn**iest** person I know.

A Copy and complete this chart.

pretty	prettiest
smelly	
moody	
gloomy	
	cheekiest
sleepy	
	messiest

B Write sentences using three of the **est** words you have made.

sp
spr

The flowers are **sprouting**. **Spring** has **sprung**.

FOCUS

KEY WORDS

spin
spot
spell
spill
spark
speak
spike
spout

spray
sprout
sprint
spring
sprang

Copy the key words neatly into your book.
Tick the ones you can find in the picture.

Lots of the key words beginning with **sp** and **spr** are hidden in this puzzle. Some go across the page and some go down.
Write them in your book.

s	p	e	a	k	s	s	p	r	i	n	g
p	x	q	e	s	p	i	l	l	o	u	x
i	m	p	s	p	r	o	u	t	a	z	r
n	l	e	s	p	a	r	k	f	t	o	p
s	p	e	l	l	y	s	p	r	i	n	t

Write three sentences. In each sentence include at least one of the words you have found.

XTENSION

The vowel letters have been left out of these sentences.
Copy the sentences neatly, putting the vowels back.

1 Th_ c_t j_mp_d _v_r th_ f_x.
2 H_ g_t cr_ss _nd r_n _ft_r th_ c_t.
3 Th_ c_t r_n _p th_ tr__.
4 "Y__ w_ll h_v_ t_ c_m_ d_wn _n_ d_y," s__d th_ f_x.

making plurals

Stroke a cat –
Stroke lots of cat**s**!

Feed a fox –
Feed lots of fox**es**!

Play with a puppy –
Play with lots of pupp**ies**!

 OCUS

 KEY WORDS

cats
girls
roads
windows
buses
bushes
churches
boxes
boys
trays
babies
hobbies

When we talk about only **one** thing it is **singular**.
When we talk about **two or more** things they are **plural**.

singular		plural
hat	+ **s** =	hat**s**
coat	+ **s** =	coat**s**

We usually add **s** to show that we mean more than one.

Write the plural of these words.

1 path   2 road   3 seat   4 pot

5 shed   6 door   7 window   8 tree

9 slug   10 cat   11 table   12 flower

EXTRA

If a noun ends with **s**, **x**, **ch** or **sh**, we add **es** to make it plural.

singular		plural
bus	+ **es** =	bus**es**
bush	+ **es** =	bush**es**

A Copy this table. Make the plural of these nouns.

singular	kiss	fox	flash	box	arch	church	brush
plural							

B Add **s** or **es** to each of these words to make them plural.

1 wish   2 car   3 class   4 street

5 fox   6 torch   7 match   8 pass

9 crash   10 passenger

EXTENSION

To make a noun plural that ends with a **y**, change the **y** to **i** before adding **es**.
But if the letter before the **y** is a **vowel** (**a e i o u**), just add **s**.

singular	plural
story	stor**ies**
day	da**ys**

Copy this table. Make the plural of these nouns.

singular	fly	hobby	valley	baby	toy	motorway	trolley
plural							

silent
b and k

lamb
knock
climb
knife
comb thumb
crumb

FOCUS

KEY WORDS

lamb
bomb
comb
climb
crumb
thumb

knee
kneel
knew
knife
knit
knot
knock

A Look at these picture clues.
Write the key words in your book.

1 l _____ 2 c _____ 3 th _____

4 k _____ 5 k _____ 6 k _____

B Underline the letters you do not hear or say when you read the words.

C Write two other silent **b** and **k** key words from each family.

Remember, a **suffix** is an ending.

XTENSION

Adding suffixes to silent **b** words is easy, like this:

comb   comb**ing**   comb**ed**

Copy and finish this chart.

comb	combing	combed
lamb		
climb		
bomb		
plumb		

Adding suffixes to silent **k** words is sometimes difficult.

Sometimes we must double the last letter before we add **ing** or **ed** or **er**.

knit   kni**tt**ing

Look at the letter before the last letter.
Is it just one vowel (**a e i o u**)?

kn**i**t   yes   kni**tt**ing
kno**c**k   no, **c** is not a vowel   kno**ck**ing

A Copy and finish this chart.

knit	knitting		
knock		knocked	knocker
knot			'
kneel			

Be careful! **Kneel** has **two** vowels before the last letter.

B Write a fun sentence that has at least four silent **k** words.

silent
W

wrap

wreck

sword

swordfish

wriggle

OCUS

KEY WORDS

wrap
wreck
write
wrinkle
wrist
wrong
wrath
wren
wrestle
wriggle
wring
whole
answer
sword

A Find nine silent **w** words hidden in the puzzle box.

a	s	w	o	r	d	j	k	p	w
g	w	r	i	s	t	f	w	w	r
w	r	e	n	w	d	e	r	h	a
h	e	w	r	o	n	g	i	o	p
i	c	n	w	r	e	s	t	l	e
q	k	o	m	d	l	c	e	e	b

B What am I?

1 I join your hand and arm.
2 I'm an old ship at the bottom of the sea.
3 I'm a very small bird.
4 I'm the solution to a question.
5 I'm an old-fashioned weapon.
6 I'm the opposite of right.
7 I'm the homophone of 'hole'.
8 I'm what you do to a parcel.

Remember, a **suffix** is a word ending.

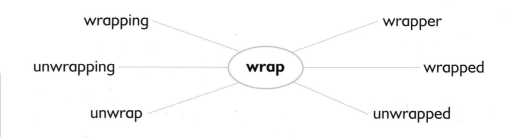

wrapping — wrapper

unwrapping — **wrap** — wrapped

unwrap — unwrapped

This web contains some of the words you can make by combining the root word **wrap** with prefixes and suffixes.

A How many other words can you make from these root words? Write them in your book. They may not have as many as **wrap**.

1 write   2 wriggle   3 wrong   4 wrestle

B Write the root word hidden in these words?

1 wholesome   2 wrecking   3 wrinkly

4 wrongfully   5 unanswerable

XTENSION

Here are some words that have other silent letters.

| column honest hour tongue |
| know knitting reign sign hymn |
| exhibit bomb climb knee knot |
| rhinoceros rhyme condemn guest |

Write these letters as headings.
Sort the words in the box into lists under the correct silent letter headings.

h   b   k   g   n   u

Add at least one more of your own words to each list. Use your dictionary to look up the meanings of any unfamiliar words.

OCUS

What are these? One letter is given to help you.
Be careful because the last three each begin with a silent letter and some of the others have silent letters, too.
Write the words in your book.

1 b_____
2 s_____
3 n_____
4 s_____

5 s_____
6 s_____
7 c_____
8 t_____

9 s_____
10 __r_____
11 __n_____
12 __n_____

A Complete these word sums, joining the root words and suffixes, changing the **y** to **i** when you need to.
Write the answers in your book.

1 beauty + ful =   2 happy + ly =   3 mercy + less =

B Add **er** to each of these words.

1 win   2 walk   3 swim   4 tank

5 stop   6 spell   7 slip   8 wrap

C Write two compound words based on each of these words.

1 time   2 thing   3 day   4 no

D Write the plural of these words.

1 shop   2 bus   3 church   4 dress   5 box

6 wish   7 story   8 battery   9 tray   10 baby

XTENSION

A Make an adjective that ends in **y** from each of these words.

1 mud   2 spot   3 rust   4 sun   5 wave

B Add **er** to each of these weather words, but be careful as one of the letters might need to be changed.

1 cold   2 stormy   3 frosty   4 cloudy

Add **est** to each of these words.

5 light   6 heavy   7 happy   8 jolly

Write a spelling rule about adding **er** and **est** to root words.

C A silent letter has been left out of each of these words. Write the words correctly in your book.

1 __rap   2 ans__er   3 s__ord   4 __nitting   5 __nock

6 __onest   7 bom__   8 si__n   9 g__est   10 __nee

one
ome
ove

Come here little white
dove, flying in the sky.
I'd love to fly
one day with you.
Oh why, oh why can't I?

KEY WORDS

gone
shone
one
done
come
some
dove
love
glove
above
shove
move
prove

Write a key word that rhymes with these.
The pictures will help you.

dove

1 _____

shove

2 _____

prove

3 _____

gone

4 _____

done

5 _____

love

6 _____

These look like magic **e** words, but they're not!
But we must still remember this rule.

When we add **ing** to a word ending in **e**, we must take off the **e**, like this:

love + ing = loving

Can you tell why these are not **magic e** words?

Add **ing** to these words.

1 love   2 move   3 shove   4 come

5 prove   6 give   7 live   8 have

XTENSION

Copy this chart.
Use the key words to help you add more words.

o says o as in dog	gone		
o says u as in sun	come		
o says oo as in moon	move		
o says its own name	hope		

words in words

me
thin
in
something
met
thing

FOCUS

KEY WORDS

that
them
then

want
what
where
when

your
because
another
something
someone
friend

Spelling is often easier if you can find small words in longer words. Copy these words and neatly underline a small word hidden in each one. The first one is done to help you.

1 be<u>cause</u>   2 what   3 friend   4 your
5 when   6 that   7 them   8 want
9 where   10 made   11 then   12 another

Write all the smaller words you can find in each of these words.
The first one is done for you.

1 carefully   *car a are ref full fully*

2 another   3 someone

4 grandmother   5 clockwise

6 unfortunately   7 forgetful

8 unsatisfactory   9 knowledge

EXTENSION

A Write your full name. Can you find any smaller words in it?

B Find a word with five smaller words within it. Write the word and the small words.

Use a dictionary to help you.

C Make word pictures to remind you how to spell these words. The first one is done to help you.

1 want

2 glove   3 string   4 shook

5 share   6 battery   7 office

aw
or ore
oor au

You've spilt the **s**a**u**ce everywhere.
It's gone all over the fl**oor**.
Bec**au**se of your carelessness
you're not having any m**ore**!

FOCUS

KEY WORDS

draw
drawer
law
torch
force
horse
Morse
sore
store
shore
moor
poor
pause

A What are they doing? Look at these picture clues.
Write the **aw** words in your book.

1 s_____ing   2 dr_____ing   3 y_____ing

4 cr_____ing   5 tr_____ing

B Write a sentence for each of the **ing** words you have written.

EXTRA

Solve these puzzles. The answers are words with **or, ore, oor, aw** or **au**.

1 it has sharp teeth, but not for eating

2 a cat has four of these

3 we do this when we feel tired

4 a loud noise from someone sleeping

5 has little money

6 to stop for a brief time

7 they work in a courtroom

8 babies do this before they learn to walk

9 you can do this with a pencil

10 this is a form of coded signal

EXTENSION

These two words have a very similar sound.

   raw   roar

They have different meanings and spellings.

Remember, words like these are called **homophones**.

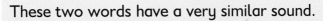

saw   sore   law   lore   paw   poor   pour

moor   more   flaw   floor   shore   sure

Choose a homophone from the box to match each clue.

1 a cat's foot

2 tipping liquid from a container

3 a grazed knee will feel like this

4 has little money

5 something you mustn't break

6 we walk all over it

7 the coastline

8 open land where sheep often graze

My dog can't stop it**ch**ing.
He can't stop scra**tch**ing.

nch
tch

FOCUS

KEY WORDS

catch
hatch
match
itch
ditch
pitch
hutch
finch
pinch
bunch
hunch
punch

A Find words that rhyme with these. The picture clues will help.
Write the answers in your book.

hatch

1 c_____

pitch

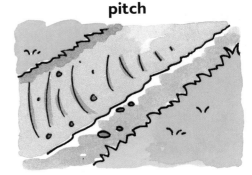

2 d_____

pinch

3 f_____

punch

4 l_____

B Write three other **tch** and three other **nch** words.

C Write a sentence that has one **tch** and one **nch** word in it.

Look at the words in the box.

snatching	scratching	sketching
stretching	stitching	switching

Find a word in the box to match each picture.

1

2

3

4

5

6

Write sentences about three of the pictures.

XTENSION

Remember, if a noun ends in **ch** we add **es** to make it plural, like this:

one match   three match**es**

Plural means more than one.

A Make these words plural.

scratch	sketch	ditch	pitch	hitch
stitch	switch	finch	bunch	lunch
	punch	bench	patch	hutch

B Say the words to yourself.
Write a sentence to explain why you think we add **es** and not just **s** to make **ch** words plural?

shortened words

It's too late! United can't make it!

F OCUS

KEY WORDS

I'm
I'll
I've
I'd
she's
he's
it's
there's
don't
isn't
doesn't
won't
can't

Write the two words that have been joined to make these words.
The first one is done to help you.

1 I'm   I am

2 I've   3 he's   4 she's   5 I'll

6 don't   7 isn't   8 there's   9 I'd

10 doesn't   11 we're   12 can't   13 won't

Remember to put the **apostrophe** where the missing letters would have been.

When two words are joined and some letters are left out, the new word is called a **contraction**.

It's is a contraction for **it is**.

An **apostrophe** (') is written where the letters have been missed out.

Copy these words and write the contraction for each pair.

1 I am   2 he is   3 is not   4 she will

5 there has   6 he would   7 do not   8 they had

9 does not   10 we have   11 will not

E XTENSION

1 Write the words that have been joined to make **can't** and **won't**. What do you notice?

2 Write two sentences, one using *there's* and one using *theirs* . Think carefully before you begin.

3 Make a list of other contractions by looking in your reading book.

mis
non ex
co anti

Don't **mis**behave.
Don't talk **non**sense.
Co-operate now!

FOCUS

KEY WORDS

misread
misplace
non-stop
non-starter
nonsense
exit
explode
co-star
co-writer
co-operate
antifreeze
antibiotic
anticlockwise

Copy and finish these word sums. The first one is done to help you.

1 mis + behave = *misbehave*

2 non + sense =

3 ex + plode =

4 co + incidence =

5 anti + biotic =

6 ex + claim =

7 anti + freeze =

8 mis + read =

9 ex + change =

Write a sentence using one of the words you have made.

Remember, a prefix is a group of letters at the beginning of a word that adds to the meaning of the word.

mis	means *wrong*
non	means *not*
ex	means *out* or *outside*
co	means *together*
anti	means *against*

You may use a dictionary to help you.

Copy these words, underline the prefixes and then write what you think the word means.

1 misfire
2 non-stick
3 excursion
4 co-star
5 anticlockwise
6 mishear
7 non-fiction
8 exit
9 co-writer
10 antifreeze
11 co-operation
12 mistake

XTENSION

Use a dictionary to help you to write four other words beginning with each of the five prefixes you have been using in this unit.
The first is done to help you.

1 mis   miscalculate   misfortune
         misinform   mistake

2 co   3 anti   4 non   5 ex

If I **could** be a wiggly worm
I **would** wriggle ar**ou**nd
in the gr**ou**nd.

ou

OCUS

 KEY WORDS

found
hound
pound
round
sound
ground

could
would
should

though
thought

A Look at these pictures. The words that go with them all rhyme with **pound**.
Write the words in your book.

1 f_____

2 r_____

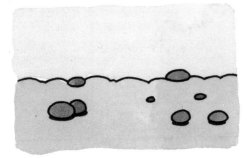

3 g_____

4 s_____

B Make a list of the key words where the **ou** letter pattern makes a different sound.

C Write a sentence that has at least two **ou** words in it.

Remember, when we make **contractions** we make one word from two

e.g. **did not** = **didn't**

Remember, sometimes we run words together as we speak.
This makes new words called **contractions**.
If we say **you** and **are** together it's written **you're**.
The apostrophe (') shows where a letter has been left out.

A Read these sentences quietly to yourself.
Try putting in **you are** or **your**. Which one makes sense?

Copy the sentences into your book, choosing *you're* (which means *you are*) or *your* to finish them.

1 Can I come to _____ party?

2 No, _____ too young.

3 I think _____ being unkind.

4 _____ wrong!

5 But _____ dad said I was old enough.

Remember to put the **apostrophe** where the missing letters would have been.

B Make contractions from these pairs of words.

1 should not   2 could not   3 would not

4 you would   5 you will   6 you have

Use each contraction in a sentence.

EXTENSION

A Look at the words in the box. Write them in alphabetical order.

| found | hound | sound |
| round | ground | pound |

B Write a definition for each word. Check what you have written by looking in a dictionary.

CHECK-UP 3

What are these? Some letters are shown to give you a clue.
Write the words in your book.

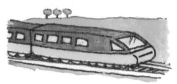

1 t _____

2 s _____ s

3 d _____

4 b _____

5 h ___ d ___

6 p _____

7 f _____

8 l _____

9 _____ h

10 s _____ g

11 __ o _____

12 __ t _____

13 ___ t ____

14 __ k _____

15 n _____ s __ .

16 __ n _____

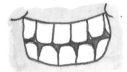

17 __ r _____

18 __ n __

19 g _____ v __

20 tr _____ r

21 h _____

22 __ a _____

23 l _____

24 p _____

EXTRA

A What is the difference between **fair** and **fare**?

B Write the plural of these words.

1 bell　　2 bus　　3 church　4 dress

5 box　　6 dish　　7 mystery　8 factory

9 play　　10 library

C Write the answers to these word sums.

1 walk + ing =　　　2 cry + ing =　　　3 slip + ing =

4 love + ing =　　　5 grumble + ed =　　6 help + ful =

7 cry + ed =　　　8 happy + ly =　　　9 mercy + less =

10 tank + er =　　　11 slow + est =　　　12 merry + er =

13 smoke + y =　　　14 heavy + est =　　　15 shake + y =

D Make another word from each of these words by adding the prefix **un**, **dis**, **de**, **re**, **mis** or **anti**.

1 frost　　2 done　　3 judge　　4 build

5 qualify　6 freeze　　7 lucky　　8 trust

E Write contractions for each of these pairs of words.

1 he is　　　2 is not　　　3 he will　　　4 there has

5 I am　　　6 she would　　7 do not　　　8 could not

9 does not　　10 would not　　11 should not　12 I would

EXTENSION

A Write your friend's full name in your book. Write all the smaller words that you can find hidden in the name.

B Write the words in each of these groups in the order they would be in a dictionary.

1 chase   duck   calf   costume

2 slippery   strong   ship   smoke   sudden

3 destroy   damp   dull   disappoint   donkey

4 apple   another   absent   adventure   altogether   agree

C A silent letter has been left out of each of these words. Write the words correctly in your book.

1 __rapper   2 ans__ers   3 s__ordfish

4 dis__onest   5 __our   6 g__ess

7 bom__er   8 si__npost   9 __now

10 ex__ibit   11 tong__e   12 r__inoceros

D Choose the correct homophone for each of these sentences.

1 I have a saw/sore toe.

2 It is against the law/lore for people under seventeen to drive a car.

3 Will you paw/poor/pour me a drink, please?

4 I'm not shore/sure what the time is.

5 Can you see the floor/flaw in this material?

6 We saw some deer running across the more/moor.